RC GWAZE

This Ain't It Chief

The Unofficial Dating Guide for Men to Be Consumed by Women

First edition

This book was professionally typeset on Reedsy.
Find out more at reedsy.com

Contents

1

Introduction

Dear men,

We have hit a wall when it comes to dating you beautiful creatures. We are tired and frustrated when it comes to dealing with your kind in this world of dating, so it's time to put the mirror up to you and show you where it's all going wrong. I know as women we're not blameless, but most romantic problems stem from you and it's time you fix up.

Love the author.

Most dating guides are long. They outline the dos and don'ts and what you as a person need to do in order to show that you are worthy of love. I think we are all worthy of love and I don't think there is a set formula in order to find it or find love adjacent companionship or sex. This dating 'guide' aims to make the ladies feel a little bit better and know that they're not alone. I will give tips to our male counterparts on the things that they really need to stop doing because they make the process longer and more difficult with their actions and I've had enough. I'll also provide some 'take at your own risk' advice to help the ladies better navigate through the piles of useless men that find themselves at our doorsteps.

I have the notion in my head that if we all start acting right then it'll be easier to find what we want. I don't think that dating secrets exist. I think there is common knowledge, common sense and gut instincts. Using those to your advantage is the best way to move forward and attempt to get out of the vicious cycle that we're currently trapped in.

Quite often, as heterosexual women dating heterosexual men, we find ourselves in situations that don't benefit us. I have realised that whether a guy starts off by ticking all the right boxes or by moving mad the outcome tends to be the same. At times it has made me wonder whether I was the problem because of the frequency of my disappointment, however talking to other females I realised it's the men we're interacting with that are problematic. No matter the circumstances, men find ways to cause unnecessary damage to a woman's romantic life by doing things that just aren't it.

The inspiration of this 'dating guide' came from a situation where a guy showed himself and it wasn't pretty. After being annoyed one too many times, I have decided that it's time to let them know what will fly and what won't. I want men to

2

know that they have been observed, analysed and evaluated. The following will be a sizing up of them and, although one size doesn't quite fit all, I think it'll be pretty close.

Throughout this 'guide', I will provide some anecdotes to show the situations that I have been through, along with the stories from other females, in order to highlight the things that heterosexual men need to stop doing. I tell these tales from a place of love and with the hopes that the men we yearn to love will listen, learn and understand. And in turn become better - at least to date.

2

But I Still Haven't Found What I'm Looking For: Reasons That We Date

The dating landscape has changed. Dating is no longer confined to solely seeking an enduring romantic relationship with someone. As maddening as that seems at times, in the modern day we've redefined what it means to be together, to love, to be loved, to have unions and companions. We're still creatures that are searching for companionship, but we're not always searching for it within the strict boundaries of conventional relationships.

Your intentions to date someone may mean that you just want to have an intimate connection and good sex. You may just want the fun of going out on dates with someone who fancies you – this is very ego driven but I don't judge. Others may be trying to figure out what they want through dating because trial and error works best for them. Others are just looking for sex, either with one person, several or anything that moves and that's also fine. Dating is not singular so the results may vary. Unfortunately, all this variation has led us to a place of confusion, perhaps ending up intertwined with people who are clearly not on the same page as us.

Ultimately, what lets us down is communication. In a world where there is no longer a singular definitive goal when it comes to dating, we are required to be better at communicating. This doesn't just mean having conversations, communicating means getting across your ideas, thoughts and feelings to the other person - something we are evidently struggling with.

SAY IT WITH YOUR CHEST!

It's essential that when we start talking to people, we let them know what we're desiring in general. Both men and women are very capable of being direct and clear. And even if you aren't necessarily sure what you're looking for from the opposite sex, it's alright to say that as well. I know a lot of people are deterred from this because of the common things we are told: 1) If you tell them you want a relationship, they'll run scared. 2) If you tell them you only want to fuck, they'll run scared. 3) If you tell them you want X, they won't even give you the time of day. Whilst this may be true at times, it isn't always. And even when it is true, why would you want someone to hang around you when their intentions aren't true?

It's fair to conclude that the problem arises when people begin to lie and when I say people, I mean men. There have been several instances where I have stated what I wanted and the person I was talking to reciprocates the same intentions, only because they think it is what I want to hear. I think too often guys lie in the dating stage. There are plenty of excuses I've heard when I've confronted guys about their lies and they're nonsensical most of the time.

I understand that guys will lie and the primary reason for lying is that it keeps you in the game a little bit longer but it's selfish. Don't let your desire get in the way of my peace. Transparency is key but is often lost because we don't want to let go of the things we desire, even if those people won't desire us as our authentic selves. Through lies and deception you waste someone else's time and that's a dickhead move. Don't be a dickhead.

As you journey through dating, you have to be open and honest. You may not always get what you want, but you'll at least be a respectable person.

Expectations vs Reality

Knowing why we've entered the dating pool is a good start, but then we need to prepare ourselves. When we know what we want, that's when we have to start thinking about our expectations and the conflict that they'll have with reality.

Sometimes we go into situations with high expectations, other times they're low and usually after dating fatigue kicks in, we go into them with no expectations. Either way, we look to the people we are interacting with in order to reasonably adjust such expectations.

Now the problem is as I've stated before, men lie. Too many guys will tell you what you want to hear when they think you want to hear it, but in all honesty the truth goes a long way. If you let me know your intentions, then I can reasonably adjust my expectations and the energy I put towards you. However, I think that guys want to receive that energy and those actions to make them feel special even if they know that they're not deserving of such energy because of the fuckery that they are bound to engage in.

I found that even when you have low expectations of men, they still want you to give so much of yourself to them. They want their cake and your cake, which quite frankly is rude. Usually there will be nothing to show for all the time and energy put into a guy, as they tend to decide whatever it is everyone wanted is no longer that they want. And they don't tend to show that they've made this decision directly, they just change their demeanour and make you feel worth a lot less than you know you are. This behaviour from the boys tends to leave us ladies deflated in the end and that's not cool.

You guys need to get your shit together, we're tired of giving to people with no intention of ever giving back. And we'd happily continue giving, if only you'd stop lying to us. I love you guys, but we deserve better than what you're currently offering. We would like to build connections with you, have joyful experiences with you, share our pain with you, understand your struggles, see your joy, partner with you, build empires with you and share this world with you.

However, we are constantly at odds when it comes to this

7

particular area in life. We're caught in a power struggle and we are hurting one another in the process. I think it's time for us heal, but in order to do that, I'm going to have to hold up a mirror up to you guys so you can see what we see, then change your behaviour to make all our lives easier.

3

Guy Profiles: The Types of Guys We Encounter

Although we lump them together often and label them as simple creatures, the guys we date come in all shapes and sizes, with varying personalities. Anything can be categorised for the sake of having a bit more clarity. I like to categorise the men, boys or guys I encounter because usually it helps me know how to best deal with them.

Dear males, after dating plenty of you and having friends who have also dated plenty of you, I want you to know that this is how we typically see you guys. There might be some categories missing, so apologies if you don't feel seen, I'm doing my best here.

The Fuckboys

First up on the list, it's the boys we know all too well. There are several types of you and I will go into greater detail because, even though you are described as a modern-day phenomenon, you have existed throughout time and I intend on doing your lineage some justice with how I describe you.

To sum you up in one sentence can be difficult at times, so I'll do it a few blanket statements:

- You do not seek encounters that are mutually beneficial for women i.e. you are self-absorbed and narcissistic.
- You are reliant on women, but seldom respect them.
- You play a lot of games rather than being straight up and honest.
- You are the men obsessed with quantity over quality i.e. it's all about how much you can get and how good it makes you feel to get it.
- No good ever comes from interacting with you boys, aside from a lesson learned.

To regard you as men feels like a degradation to the word because you act with little to no emotional intelligence and have a lot of growing up to do, hence the term, fuck**boy**.

Now, do I think that you are bad people? No, like everyone else you are flawed people, but you definitely do more bad things than good when it comes to interpersonal romantic relationships.

Types of Fuckboys

- **Legitimate Young Professional:** You've recently graduated (give or take five years) and you have a technically worded graduate job that most likely requires you to do basic things like sit at a desk, type and send emails. You are set on getting rich and buying dumb stuff. Women to you are just an accessory. You will claim that you don't have time for relationships because you're busy with your career goals and you'll use that as an excuse to plough through as many girls that are attracted to the shiny objects you've obtained such as your car and/or watch. There'll be one or two girls who you actually like because you're not immune to feelings (despite how much you claim to be), but your way of functioning means you will hurt these girls by being bad at communicating, bad at prioritising and infidelity of some kind. Despite knowing this about yourself you still seek companionship with girls because you love attention and feeling as important as your job title makes you feel.

· **Illegitimate Young Professional:** You are either a drug dealer or a fraud guy. You have a similar attitude and approach to women as your legitimate counterparts. The fact that you endanger them with your schemes alone shows that you're not serious. You'll similarly catch feelings at times, but you'll be incapable of treating the girl right. You are often distant, busy trying not to get caught and you'll be entertaining other girls who are fascinated by your bad boy vibes (not typically applicable for the fraud boys). You've bought into the mentality of having a ride or die but haven't put in the work to make sure you can even sustain a relationship. Also, with you ride or die could literally mean

11

die and that's extremely not cool.

· **Pretty Boys:** You guys know you are good looking and that gives you confidence. Your confidence radiates and women are drawn to you. Knowing this puts you at an advantage because you know how to get the girls you want and even keep around the girls you don't want. You love the attention and you've got a half decent personality, so you excel in the dating game. You're dangerous and you've broken your fair share of hearts. You're even more problematic because you apologise so well – not even sincerely, just so well – that the women you hurt can't stay mad at you. You often create situations with girls where they'll close their door but leave a window open for you...you're lethal.

· **Entertainers:** You have access to plenty of women and they usually know how to get access to you. Like the pretty boys, you play on your position of power and use to get what you want. You are dangerous and usually noncommittal. When you do commit, you come with a lot of heartbreak and infidelities. You are not practical men to date, but your sex appeal means we will make room for your fuckery in our lives, even against our better judgment. Plus, you apologise like your pretty counterparts, hard to resist and risky at best.

· **Emotionally Castrated and Horny:** You are incapable of making connections with others. This comes from emotional trauma you clearly haven't healed from, and you show no signs of ever getting better. You treat women simply as bodies rather than people. Your approach with some is brazen and they accept that you are a dickhead, but your post-sex catharsis will manipulate them into thinking you have a little bit of a heart, meaning they'll excuse your mistreatment of them. With other ladies you lie your way into their beds and pretend you're not an awful guy to date because you can tell who will give you the time of day and who won't - you're clever like that. When people approach you again, to let you know that you've hurt them, you shrug it off and say that they knew what you were like when they got acquainted with you, but did they really? No. Lying and manipulation are your sports and you most likely need therapy. Something in you needs reconciling.

· **Unsure and Horny:** You don't know what it is you want exactly and it's problematic. Often you just let your hormones take over, so even in situations where you were doing well in terms of getting to know someone and like them, you opt for the 'less complicated' route where you decide to nut then leave. You are capable of connecting, but you make rash decisions based on what you want in the moment and then you end up hurting others in the process. At the end of the day you are immature and selfish. You need to get yourself together before you start approaching the ladies, sir. It's for the best.

13

· **I Don't Want You But No One Else Can Have You:** The idea of commitment scares you, but you want someone to be devoted to you. There's a girl you met some time ago and she's great - in all honesty - she's perfect. But like I said, you can't commit. You play games with her; you tell her things aren't working and eventually she learns to accept how you are. Occasionally, she'll meet new people who are on the same wavelength as her in terms of what they want, and this is when your storm back into her life. Like a hurricane you come and devastate her peace. You lead her into thinking that you've changed, but realistically you don't want to see her with someone else. You are territorial, selfish and childish. Leave her alone unless you learn to commit please, she can do better than you.

· **Can't Get Girls but Is Still A Fuckboy:** Even some of the unluckiest fools will move mad. I'm pretty sure you know which guys I'm talking about. It's not just about body counts, it's just a mentality. Some guys have a fuckboy mentality, but they lack the capability to pull it off. You guys are the ones that try moving to girls, get rejected then turn around and call the same women sluts or whores. You have very little game and tend to take it out on women because they see through you and are not interested. You need to learn to respect women and quite frankly, grow the fuck up.

Signs That You're a Fuckboy

1. You fit the profile of the fuckboys labelled above (See **Types of Fuckboys**).
2. You only want to see a girl when it's late. You are not a vampire. If you want to see me, then you best vary the hours of the day and also be mindful that I have a sleeping pattern, sometimes a girl is out by ten.
3. You only want to see a girl in close proximity to a bed. Similar to sign number 2 but based more on location than time of day. If you want to see me, then vary the places which we meet at. Maybe I want to go for a walk in the park or for a nice cocktail. Variety is the spice of life and trying to constantly direct me to the space of your bed is boring.
4. You always approach girls with nonspecific plans. This is a minor, but there are different vibes when you ask a girl to 'hang' over a specific date activity. Chances are you haven't actually told this girl you only want to smash and you're stringing her along. Also, on top of that these nonspecific plans don't include a time and place, therefore when you ask you're expecting someone to just be available to you. We need a power balance not a power trip.
5. You lie about your dating life. If we ask you specific questions, it's not because we're insecure, it's just because we want to know where we stand and act in accordance to the information you provide. If your responses are "you don't need to worry about that" or "why are you stressing?", it's most likely because you're up to no good. Just be honest and see if I'm game for the situation you desire for us. Let me make fully formed decisions, just like I allow you to do with me.
6. You do frequent disappearing acts. There's nothing more suspect than a guy that falls off the face of the earth for

a solid week or two. If we're dating and you disappear like that, you are definitely leading a double life. It's not everyday text, I get that. Sometimes life is boring, and you've got nothing new to say or sometimes you don't want to talk to anyone, but a text here and there to say you're alive is the least you can do. If you're with your family (wife and kids) though, delete my number, let me live a quiet life because I don't want to fight your wife.

7. You say you like a girl but ghost after nutting. Too often guys will lie until a girl finally sleeps with them. If you've done this then just know, you are truly awful and need to change your ways. At least be honest at the end of the day and say it's not what you want rather than to just flat out ignore someone. It's uncouth and distasteful.

8. You objectify women at a very high level. Objectification of men and women is more common in our society due to the changing views on sex. Talking about the ways in which we admire the body of the opposite sex is usually fine, but objectification is taking it that one step further and dehumanising the people we're talking about. If all you can say about the women you see is, "what a pair of tits" or "look at the size of that bum" then you're most likely a fuckboy. There is room for sexual desires, but objectification is a **no no**.

9. You want to nut in every girl you meet. Nutting really isn't that deep, there's more to life than sex. I think you might need new hobbies or sex therapy.

10. You have to avoid certain locations because you've fraternised with the women there and they hate you or are too comfortable with you. Having to avoid clubs, bars, coffee shops, supermarkets, leisure centres and other public

places because your dick has tainted them all is definitely a sign that you're a fuckboy. If you avoid them specifically because you want to avoid hostility, then you know that where your dick goes, animosity follows and that's not a good thing. You're destroying your own peace and you should probably apologise.

11. You lie and you just can't seem to stop. Lying is probably the greatest signifier of a fuckboy. Being a fuckboy is rooted in lying to yourself and others in order to fulfil your desires.

12. Your interests in women revolve around you and what you can get from them, not what you can provide for them. You are solely seeking experiences with women for your benefit alone. It's all one-sided.

13. You do not care whether someone gets hurt or not. The feelings of the women you interact with are not at the forefront of your mind when you make decisions that affect them. Where's your sense of empathy? MIA, that's where!

14. Someone has directly said you are a fuckboy. Chances are they are not wrong. They've probably assessed your behaviour and have seen key fuckboy traits within you.

Just to be clear, dating multiple people doesn't make you a fuckboy. If you are honest with your movements, are clear with your intentions, and you show that you actually care for and respect the people you are dealing with, then that is fine. My only advice on that is that you don't wear yourself out and spread yourself too thin dating multiple people. Trust me, it's not fun after a while.

As stated, it's the dishonesty, narcissism, disrespect and using of other people that makes one a **fuckboy.** And yes, women can do the same thing too, but this is not about us, it's about you!

Fuckboy Tales

Sorry to that girl:
   "Sometimes a girl just wants to have fun. I met a guy at a party, took him back to my place and we slept together. It was all fun and games until afterwards he asked me not to tell anyone. Naturally, I asked why, and it was because he had a girlfriend, so I kicked him out! Sorry to that girl, though, he didn't mention you all those hours before."

Anyone got pen and paper:
   "My friend with benefits in my first year at university had a whole ass secret girlfriend the entire time we were seeing each other. It was an open relationship so maybe that's why he didn't feel the need to say anything until one night I was out. I saw him and we exchanged pleasantries as usual then he had the nerve to tell me that he couldn't come back with me that night – as if I'd even asked – because his girlfriend was out with him and staying for the weekend. In addition, she wasn't pleased at the number of girls he'd been approached by that same night. I heard it through the grapevine that she argued with him asking him to write down all the girls he'd slept with so far. I think the relationship was more open on one side than it was on the other, but that's none of my business." *sips

tea*

Trust no one:
"I was in a situationship with a guy, so obviously I wasn't very territorial, but we tried to be respectful and had set some boundaries, for example, I couldn't flirt with his boys and what not. Anyways, early on in our dealings, I found out that he was receiving nudes from one of my opps – an opp is an enemy basically. He initially denied it, but eventually came clean and claimed I was the only one he was dealing with after that incident. In general, he infuriated me but the sex was really good so I dealt with him for longer than I should have. Here's the kicker, I found out several months after we'd stopped dealing with one another that he'd been sexual with one of my close friends during the same time period."

Persistence is not always key:
"I had a very casual and brief fling with a guy but after a few weeks we called it off because he was starting to get serious with someone else. I accepted it and moved on like any reasonable fuck buddy would. Then, over a month later, I saw him at a festival, and he was dangerously flirty with me, so I assumed he was longer seeing the other girl. Then, after I left him, he texted me letting me know how much he wanted me. Later on that night, I saw him in a queue and he called me over to apologise as he revealed he was still seeing that girl. I accepted the apology, told him to be respectful of what he had and enjoy it. But of

course, he had to tell me how much he wanted to kiss me before I left him just to make things awkward. Either you're committed to her or you're not, please leave me out of it."

Wasted time and abused empathy:

"I've had a lot of timewasters and it'd be a dissertation if I were to go through all of them and their shortcomings, but alas, I'll discuss one that is fresher in memory. This tale begins with little ol' me talking to a guy for about 3 weeks and the two of us arranging a date. All was going well, we both seemed excited and we'd confirmed where to meet, but we were going to clarify the time in the morning based on his commute to the location – he lived a bit further out than me. The morning arrived, so I shot him a text when I woke up, but I got radio silence. I texted a few more times an hour or so later, only to get no response and I even called him to see what was going on, but I got nothing. So, the date didn't occur and little ol' me was upset because I was excited, but I was also mad that I wasn't given any warning or an explanation. He resurfaced a few days later, all apologetic and blaming either his work or mother or both. He talked me back into sweetness saying all the right things and I expressed that moving forward the communication had to be open and honest; he agreed, I forgave, and we arranged another date. Leading up to this one I was a bit wary, but of course I still wanted to maintain the excitement, but the night before he messaged me to cancel, this time using his mother and a doctor's appointment as excuses. I took

it on the chin and was understanding, but of course the feeling that he didn't want to see me grew. However, he apologised emphatically stating that that the next date we make he will definitely show up to and he'll make it the best I have ever had in order to make up for disappointing me twice. So, once again we planned a date, with an agreed place and time, so it was just a matter of getting ready and going to meet. On the day, I got ready and sent a couple messages his way just to make sure he was still alright with our plans and yes, you guessed it...I got nothing back. Then once again I called him only to get no response. There I was, all ready to go for a date and he wasn't picking up. This time there was no room for sadness, just anger, so I messaged him letting him know that what he did wasn't cool and that if he didn't want to see me, he never has to. I got no response; it was about a week later he messaged letting me know he was sorry. At this point sorry meant fuck all, but in the spirit of not holding grudges, I forgave him, especially since he confided in me about his depression causing him to freak out before all the dates and he feared the rejection. To his confiding I was kind and I reciprocated the trust by letting him know that I too go through the same thing, but there's healthy ways to cope with it that don't involve hurting other people. He seemed to understand that, or at least I thought he did, until we arranged another date, the day came, and he did it again. I really tried with this one. I was very understanding of everything and was never rude, even though his behaviour was unacceptable. I understand mental health is a challenge, but it isn't an excuse to treat people like this. If you cannot

21

reciprocate the open and honest communication, just let me know and I'll go. I'm mainly mad that my empathy and understanding was abused so many times by one guy. I was a bit of a mug and he was a fuckboy for sure, he really didn't care about my feelings and apologised well enough to put me through it time and time again."

Duped, hoodwinked, bamboozled:

"I spent over two months getting to know a guy I matched with on Bumble. From day one we were doing video calls and just being honest and upfront, just not to waste time. We got into a habit of at least three video calls a week and had a level of communication that worked for us. The vibes were good and neither of us were seeking a relationship, so we were happy with the chill dynamic we had established. After two plus months we met up and finally had sex. It was great to say the least, but from that point on things got a bit weird. He started being distant and told me that he might not be as easy to reach anymore. I was a bit confused, but just continued with my life as usual. He contacted me again after about 3 weeks to check in on me (he only checked in on me because racism was on the forefront of the news and probably wanted to tick off 'check on a black person' on his anti racism list). After that I didn't hear from him, even though I'd sent him a message that concerned both of us, so I decided that I would delete all trace off him from my phone in order to just move on. As I was doing my last bit of deleting all trace of him, I thought to check his Instagram one last time and through a little bit of browsing I found out that

the reason he had sacked me off was because he was back with his ex-girlfriend, something I feel like he could have told me. However, my gut told me that maybe there was more to the story and she was right. I told my girlfriends and they did some deep diving on my behalf as I was too livid to look again. They informed me that the dates didn't add up and we found out that I was definitely a side hoe. When he'd spoken about his 'ex' he'd expressed that he'd been a serial cheat throughout their relationship, so maybe that should have been my cue to run, but also he'd said that he'd changed, and that's the reason he'd chosen to be 'single'. I really believed everything he said and in the end I got played. I mean I just wanted a simple, low strings attached relationship with an attractive and interesting guy, it's just a shame the guy I'd chosen wasn't actually single. What a lying prick!"

The Nice Guys

This is a branding that conflicts me because the bar is so low, that the things you should just be doing are seen as extraordinary, therefore, your basic manners become the whole personality trait. It's just a bit wild if you ask me! If I were to rebrand, I'd probably call you the safe guys, the more predictable guys, the guys less likely to play games and sometimes the more boring guys (this is a more person-dependent description).

Being nice is a good and admirable trait. I really value men who move with understanding and compassion. The ability to be selfless and value the needs of the person you are interested in is appreciated and definitely something we all should have. However, there is more to a person than their ability to be nice and that's where the nice guys falter.

People are complex creatures and if you hide the other parts of yourself all for the sake of an image, then you'll be in for a reckoning when the cracks start to show. Obviously, don't turn around and suddenly be mean for no reason, but don't take shit every day. If we're dating and I annoy you, let me know. I won't think you're not nice afterwards, you can be nice as well as honest. This false persona needs to go because amongst the majority of us no one is that nice all the time. There are very few exceptions.

Another pet peeve when it comes to the nice guy is expectation and entitlement. Some men think that because they treat women in a certain manner, they are entitled to certain aspects of said woman. Firstly, matters of the heart aren't solely transactional. It's not a case of I did this for you, so I deserve that. Secondly, you can't pin your expectations of how you think someone should react and then act out when they don't behave or act in a certain manner. It's like when you rehearse a conversation in your head and it doesn't go the way you planned, you don't get mad at the other person for that and state you deserve a better conversation than they gave you. So why is it that Nice Guys feel the need to state that you should have been more grateful for them not treating you like shit? It's honestly just manipulative. Using your track record is manipulation and definitely shows that you're not always nice, hence why I dislike the label.

Additionally, nice guys are also the guys whose personalities may not shine, so the only thing we can attribute to them is being nice. Now I don't want every guy who's been labelled a Nice Guy to worry, because not all of you are boring, however, some of you need to work on your personality so we have more interesting things to say about you.

I have no nice guys stories because they'll probably just bore you. I'm joking, I have at least one nice guy story in the vault, but the guy depicted borders on socially inept as well.

Yes, you're lovely, but slow your roll and listen dude:

"Even the nicest of guys have their flaws and unfortu-nately, I had to deal with a boy, who was very pleasant in many respects, but overthought it and developed a very quick fixation with me. Now 15-year-old me would have loved that sort of attention, but having grown a lot since then and established boundaries for myself, there's certain behaviours that I just can't deal with. The boy was so sweet, and it was easy to be around him at first. However, by declaring such emphatic like for me and stating he wanted me to be his girl, despite me saying I'd like to take things slow, I definitely felt uncomfortable. His actions and words were not in line with my boundaries and I felt like I was saying things and he was half listening. When I broke things off with him, I was very clear, but of course he was baffled because he'd treated me well unlike some of the guys I'd mentioned from the past – do I smell at attempt at manipulation? He really tried to use my

past against me so that I'd keep him around – not cool. This move blinded him from seeing that the problem was his intensity towards me and nothing else. Trying to get to know someone who's put you on a pedestal is a lot to deal with and it's awkward. I stand by my statement that he's a nice guy, not bottom barrel like some of the other guys I have encountered, but the hints of entitlement and not being aware of my boundaries was a major no. He moved a bit mad for me in that situation."

The Funny Guys

You're honestly our favourites, as long as you're not also a Fuckboy. We love to be entertained and that's why we gravitate towards you, even when you're not the hottest in the room. Where you don't give us a burning desire to rip off your clothes there and then, you fill it with a laughter that makes us want to slowly undress you.

Your humour is part of an undeniable charm and we do value you for it, but sometimes you neglect the need to be serious. Not all situations call for laughter, and sometimes we need you to tap into your other emotions. It's okay to show more than one side of yourself boys, I already told the Nice Guys this.

Hot but Dead Personality Guys aka Vampires

Physical attraction is usually what first draws us in. It's a really nice feeling to meet someone who is universally hot and isn't rude. However, we can't have it all. Sometimes being attractive means you don't work on your personality and this leads to becoming a one-dimensional character with little to no opinions or basic interests i.e. you love the gym, FIFA and COD.

As Hot Guys, you will provide the looks but most of the time when you engage in conversation it will be boring and lacklustre. I call you vampires because you will suck the life and soul out of me with useless, skin deep responses. Now, boring is subjective, but when people are limited to small talk, we can all agree that they probably don't have much else to say and when lust and intellect battle, intellect wins usually. Do take pride in your looks whilst they last since they will fade away and maybe pick up a new hobby or two - gain some depth.

The Weirdos

Some guys have a certain air about them and will come as across as weird. From socially inept to creepy, we have the category of the weirdos.

Socially Inept

There are things that you don't do, social cues that you should understand and things you definitely don't say. I'm not sure if it's just their nature or if it's nurture that causes some guys to be extremely socially inept. It is usually not your intention to offend or make women uncomfortable, but you just do sometimes. It's something we pity, but after a while it's annoying and needs to be fixed.

Maybe you don't have enough women in your lives, therefore, when we approach you only have dumb shit to say. There's also the possibility that you are shy and have friends who are also inexperienced in matters of romance, so you can't seek their advice on how to function. It's also likely that you're young and inexperienced so most things you say and do are still playground based. Your limited social adaptation means that you ask the oddest things or simply do them without the realisation that maybe, just maybe, it's a bit weird. We can only forgive you so much, so you need to start learning how not to be so odd and infuriating.

Make it make sense please:

"There once was a boy who came in saying that he wasn't like the others and he was right for me. I think he meant he was a lot more intense than the others and I'll tell you why. From day one he was going hard on wanting to be my guy, even though we'd only started talking. From wanting me to only date him only after talking one day and being adamant that I'd be happy as his girlfriend, even though I hadn't yet met him, I knew I had a mad one on my hands. I'm not sure why this has occurred more to me recently, but some guys need to learn that we all have processes and I told him mine, but he chose to ignore it and kept pushing for me to be his girlfriend without having even met. What made the situation more awkward was

*one day I found myself blocked from his account and he came back the next day stating it was his ex that did it. Now, I can never know the full truth, but the toxicity of his past relationship was jumping out at me and I wanted to get out. I did manage to successfully remove myself, but of course I wasn't able to escape the petty comment of "you don't know what you're missing out on, I would've treated you like a queen". Was I supposed to fawn and claim you as my king? Hell to the fucking no. Allow me to leave peacefully, your obsession with me is a **you** problem, and **you** need to fix it."*

Creepy

These are the guys that are fully aware of their words and actions and the consequences those may carry but choose to ignore them. It's like making you uncomfortable is their calling and they'll do an array of things to gain your attention.

You are a Creepy Guy if you typically send girls inappropriate and uncomfortable messages, catcall or honk your horn at girls on the streets or give unwanted physical contact to girls – especially in clubs (there's no reason your hand needs to go on my waist to get past me in a club, ever!). Your actions are egregious, and you should be ashamed of yourselves. Do better.

Creep Alert:
   "The first guy I ever slept with took my knickers from that night and then told me he still had them in his top drawer like a year later. I really didn't need to know that

information."

Controversial Opinions Guys

They think unpopular opinions are a personality trait. They have a tendency to be misogynistic, homophobic, racist, xenophobic, classist or any other kind of **ist** or **ic** there is. Typically, they are one incident away from being banned from an online platform or becoming an incel. If this is you then you probably need some form of therapy to reconcile whatever is broken inside you. It's not the fault of women that they're repulsed by you, the things you say and the things you do. It's just you sir.

Know your audience, but I'm glad he showed himself on the first date:
"I once went on a date with a guy who was 'exclusively into black girls' – I know that should've been my red flag. We were getting on fine, but then after seeing something on the screen of the bar that we were in, we had a debate. He tried to tell me that black people weren't oppressed and that we were just to hypersensitive to people's comments. I really had to spend half the date talking about my experiences with overt and subtle racism, which wasn't fun and still he concluded black people were 'too sensitive'. This really wasn't it and definitely not worth two drinks. Safe to say I never saw him again and I hope no black woman ever does."

The Guys Cheating on Their Girlfriends Overtly i.e. they'll even cheat in front of her.

This man is a walking talking red flag. He is a fuckboy in all honesty, toxic to the core. He has unresolved emotional issues and if you are him, go seek therapy. This level of toxic behaviour is wild and does all the harm and no good at all.

Ladies, avoid this man if you see him and if you're already with him, leave him sis. He's not changing any time soon. And if this is you, please get the help that you need.

The Guys Cheating on Their Girlfriends Secretly i.e. we won't know she exists until we do a CRB.

I'm sure several ladies have been in these situations where they're dating a guy, and all is going well. Then we do a CRB check and find out you have a girlfriend, fiancé or even a wife. I have not experienced the wife or fiancé – I do know some people that have – but I have experienced being the other woman, completely by accident. It's great for you that you've been blessed with the talent to conceal major aspects of your life, that's quite the skill. I wish you'd use your skills to work for MI6 or some other intelligence organisation rather than to break hearts.

A side hoe kind of year:
"It came to my attention that a lot of guys like to hide their girlfriends. In one year I found out that five guys I

had started dating or had slept with, turned out to have girlfriends. One of those five, I had a threesome with so he technically cheated on his girlfriend with me and his boy. Another one was in bed with me when he answered and call from his girlfriend of four years. I sat there absolutely horrified as he pretended like I wasn't there."

Sex, lies and a birthday weekend:
"So, I'd been seeing this guy for about four months. We met at work. At the time he'd told me that'd he'd recently broken up with his girlfriend, so I wasn't expecting something serious and to be honest I'd only been single for a few months, so I wasn't looking for anything major either. The dick was good, and the company was alright. I was a little bit dubious of his past relationship as in my CRB his ex still had their images up, but he assured me it was over and that she was just finding it hard to move on. On top if that, he was very clingy and would talk about us as if we were in a sort of relationship and even planned aspects of 'our future'. He was a bit much, but the good dick had me just going along with it all. Then on the weekend of my birthday, four months into seeing him, he'd decided he wanted to spend the weekend with me and make it special. I was apprehensive at first since days before I'd had a dream where his ex had come to me and stated they were still together, call it a premonition, I guess. The weekend arrives and he comes over. After I thought he'd finished bringing his stuff in, he says he's forgotten something in the car and goes back to it. After about half an hour I get a bit concerned because he hasn't come back yet, so I message him to check if things are

alright. I get nothing. I call him a few minutes later and again, nothing. Then I look outside, and I see him. At this point he's sitting in his car with his supposed ex-girlfriend. I then get a Facebook message from this girl asking how I know him. I decide not to answer because I really don't know what's going on and also, she's outside my house which is quite unsettling. I call him again; I can fully see him as well but still he doesn't pick up. They drive off shortly afterwards as I just stand there looking out. I hear nothing from him for hours, but the girl messages me again and lets me know that she has just discovered that her boyfriend is cheating on her with me and that they didn't break up in January like he said. He had actually been with her that very morning and she'd only come to my house because he'd lied about where he was which had made her suspicious, and he'd taken their car to come and see me. All this time he'd been leading a double life, lying to her and me. That's how my birthday weekend started, how fab! But he did give me the gift of his humiliated face when I assisted his ex in kicking him out. Safe to say he wasn't expecting to see me there."

How Do We Remedy This?

Well it's simple, we don't. We can't change you and people only change if they are willing to. Individuals need to do the work in order to become better people and in turn it should make them easier to date. However, these profiles should help you, as

33

heterosexual men, see how we see you and maybe prompt you to start doing the work or at least stop lying to us and yourselves. And of course, for us women, we can start identifying the guys we pick and run if we're interacting with a profile that we know will do us all the harm, and no good.

4

Ways to Meet: The Real World to the Online

Friends to Lovers

How often this happens is unbeknown to me. Often the story is a guy doesn't want to be more than friends with a girl due to fear that it will ruin the friendship if things don't work out. This narrative of friends becoming lovers is often a cinematic one, but sometimes it does occur.

It is possible to forge a romantic relationship from a friendship, but I think most people avoid it, even though I think these types of relationships have more potential to thrive. I think the idea of knowing someone so well then proceeding to date them can feel a bit weird, but it has its advantages for sure. Personally, I only like all my male friends as just friends and I hope that's how they see me too, it's hard to chat shit about your man if you've known how he is for the longest time and you have the same friends.

Meeting Through Friends/Setups

Oh, to have friends who have attractive friends, that must be nice. This is another method of meeting someone new for a romantic situation that I attribute heavily to cinema. I can count the number of times my friends have set me up with someone on zero fingers and the times I have introduced a friend of mine to someone I know on one.

I understand that there's an awkwardness in being the middleman between people you know, so that is probably why not many people meet in that manner. However, I think maybe we should try introducing people who we think would vibe more often and see if they hit it off. Let's make this a more popular way of meeting.

Also, if you're a guy and I'm friends with one of your friends and you think that I'm attractive, convince our mutual friend to set up something so that we can meet. I'm open to this avenue of introduction; I just can't promise that I'll be attracted, like you or even fall in love with you, but I'm open to the idea.

The Workplace

Now I have never had a workplace romance, because I don't like to 'shit where I eat'. The closest I ever got to that was hooking up with a co-worker once and till this day I regret the awkwardness that brought me for my final few shifts.

Often when I hear about workplace romance, it honestly scares me. Mixing business and pleasure often leaves people bitter. I have a friend who works in HR and I'm sure when they receive those forms stating that two employees are in a relationship they must sigh to high heaven.

However, my personal discomfort should not discourage you from shooting your workplace shot. More often than not you'll have things in common and conversation topics just from the workplace alone, but obviously don't oversaturate your conversations with work. If it works for you then all the best but keep it appropriate in the workplace for the sake of everyone else.

In Da Club/Or Bar

You never know who you'll encounter when you leave the house and go to these social settings. Typically, you're out with your friends having a good time, but some sultry eye contact with a hot stranger can definitely change the course of your night and spice up your life.

Meeting new people can be a part of going out and meeting attractive people is definitely considered a highlight. However, in these spaces, the people we meet are usually charged up with substances and hormones. The people we meet here don't tend to be for a long time; it's usually for a good time – yeah, I know I said it and I kind of regret it, but it is pretty much the truth.

It is definitely romanticised in the world of film and television, where people meet in these places and forge everlasting connections, but realistically you'll end up with texts asking, "who's this?", someone sneaking out of your house at 4AM or crying in the club.

Don't go crying in the club:

"I actually had a whirlwind romance with a guy I met in a club. It's a bit of a long story, but I need to justify the tears I cried when it abruptly ended. I was on my favourite night out of the week. My mood was on 10 and I was dancing with the girls, very carefree and unbothered. He caught my eye, from a short distance away; my friend had actually clocked him looking at me for a while. In our own secret coding, I asked her what she thought, and she gave me the green light, so I signalled him over. Once he approached, I danced with him for a while and eventually our lips collided. At this point we were really feeling each other, and I mean FEELING! Before things got too heated, we decided to take a moment off the dance floor and actually find out the basic information such names, age and student courses etc. By the end of the conversation we pretty much knew we were going home with one another at the end of the night. I mean the physical attraction was there, the pheromones were jumping and in between the compliments he was giving me, he was telling me that he doesn't usually pick up girls this way and he wanted to also take me on a date. I had an unwillingness to trust a guy in a club, so I reacted in a blasé manner to his comments. I half believed him, and half didn't. When we were finally alone, in my room and he was not quick to

*undress me. He was actually quite shy, and we spent about
30 minutes talking instead of rushing to get to the sex part.
It was quite nice to be experiencing a very sweet boy. We
took our time, then finally got into it and throughout it
all he was constantly checking in and asking if things
were okay, which I really appreciated. After the deed was
done, we exchanged more stories and we dove deeper into
our lives. By the end of the night we'd arranged a date
and he'd taken things an extra step further by already
making plans for second and third dates. In my head I
was like 'whoa, slow down', but he was unlike any guy
I'd met so far so I just let it slide. Within hours of saying
goodbye, we met up for a date where I cooked for him
and it was really cute. He also met a few of my friends –
not by force, but just because of location. After that date,
we spent a couple of days straight together just enjoying
one another's company. In these meetings, he was so
adamant on me meeting his friends and even his family.
He'd started to plan how he could come and visit me at
home whilst we were on summer break and how I could
do the same. We were trapped in a very intense bubble,
but like I said, whirlwind romance. It was exciting. He
excited me. He told me all the things many girls want to
hear, so eventually I was like 'Okay, I can get on board
with his plan. He's clearly into me, he says he's proud to
show me off. His palms get a little bit sweaty when he
holds my hand because he's nervous. Plus, we have a lot
in common, it's easy to get along with him and my friends
find him pleasant so what could go wrong?'. No one had
really shown such emphatic like and commitment like
he had, so I decided to enjoy everything he was giving to*

me. And all was well. All was well until it wasn't. It took one night, one kiss and then he backtracked. I finally got on board, he kissed another girl – well she kissed him – but they stayed talking the entire night and I was upset because I'd been on the receiving end of HIS plans for us. Then after that incident, it was all of a sudden too much for him, he wasn't ready for a relationship and somehow, I was forcing it on him. I was baffled by the 180 and this was my first real taster in the madness of men. He had sold me a dream and by the time I bought into it, he'd decided that it was out of stock. The thing is on the night of the incident, we had an argument and took a few days to cool off and get back into the swing of things. He actually decided to dump me about a week later in the very place that we had met, on my favourite night out. So yeah, that was the reason I was crying in a club, whilst trying to stop my angry friend from fighting the boy, because she was mad that he had hurt me."

Online Dating Apps

If you haven't been here, then count yourself lucky. This is where hopes of love and union go to die. All the types of guys mentioned in Chapter 2 exist here because it is the real world condensed into applications on your phone. The 'singles' out there and I say that loosely (see **Chapter 2**) will present themselves in different ways depending on the app they use.

The apps are the new norm, so at least people no longer send dumb messages saying, "we'll say we met in the supermarket". There's no shame which is good, but also there's NO SHAME. When it comes to conduct, there is no shame. The lack of accountability in this realm is probably the most off-putting aspect of it. I honestly have had some atrocious experiences with online dating. The sites may vary but the guys are the same, therefore, so are the results.

There is very little reward and quite a bit of risk, we don't have many options so here we are. Please try not to infuriate us during our time here, be respectful and don't move mad.

He really didn't get it:

"I matched a boy on Hinge and after some brief conver-sations, I let the guy know I wasn't feeling him because I'm not for leading boys on for attention anymore – #mature. Then he had the nerve to start asking invasive shit such as, 'Do you have sex on the first date?' Excuse you sir, you've just been rejected, you are not getting a first date, stop being invasive. I decided I would check him for being a chauvinistic pig but still politely because I won't let all the growth that I've had go just because the boys are moving mad. His response to this brief schooling I gave him was 'but babe I like you', like that meant shit to me. Then the same guy who I had clearly told I wasn't interested, came back a few weeks later and like all narcissistic pricks, he thought to message me asking that I go for drinks with him. I politely refused and stated that it was futile as we didn't want the same things and

also, I didn't want to waste my time and money. The only justification he had for it being a good idea for ME was that HE found ME attractive. I was baffled, how does YOUR attraction for ME, translate into us going on a date? I once again politely set him straight and thought, okay we're done here, but no his dumb mouth decides to ask if I want something casual with him like friends with benefits. Now, I'm steady like 'can you read?', I don't want YOU in any capacity, we're not friends and I've rejected you more times in these messages than I've had dates all year. He claimed to not understand why I wasn't interested in his proposal and started ranting at me about my purpose on the dating app, Hinge (which I deleted soon after my first interaction with him). I had to tell him that you can be on dating apps for whatever reason you like and you're allowed to say it to the people you encounter – which I'd done with him more than once, but apparently not as many times as I should have because he was clearly dropped on his head. I decided to read him one last time and let him know he's not entitled to me or my time and that he needed to grow up. After that he still didn't get the message, because responded with 'but I still like you'. There was no getting through to him, so the final option was to block him. . The moral of this story is that you are not entitled to anyone and if they tell you to leave them alone, do so. The romanticising of persistence has led to guys moving mad and just making people feel uncomfortable. Also, I learned from this encounter that no matter how much you try and educate someone, it won't always sink in, so you're better off protecting your peace and just blocking. Don't try and paint the red flag green, just toss it into the fire."

Proper Online Dating i.e. you pay for this shit

I guess this is the nicer version of the hell that is the apps, but the dance is all the same. Getting to know people through the online medium can be limiting and when you finally meet in person you might have just wasted your time and money. It's a method of meeting someone that requires patience, willingness and open-mindedness.

This is for the serious people who are invested in finding something more definitive as opposed to the app inhabitants. I have never ventured on these sites, so I really don't know what they are saying, but I assume they have their pros and cons like every other methods of meeting people. The pros including that men exist on them and the cons being that very same thing.

5

Online Dating Apps: How to Market Yourselves Well and Not Be Creepy

The purpose of this guide is to provide stories that give teachable moments; however, I think when it comes to this area, I just need to give some straight up advice.

A lot of guys complain how easy it is for girls to accumulate matches and be exposed to more people to get to know. Whilst this is statistically true, it doesn't mean that much, after all, it's quality over quantity boys. The numbers are purely just ego and exercising options you probably don't wish to take. I'll refrain from getting too preachy here and just give you the advice you're looking for when it comes to creating attractive profiles.

It's a game of marketing. You are a product and you want the ladies to invest in you. In order for them to buy, they have to be attracted to the packaging, see the potential benefits of having the product in their life and have the confidence that it will be a reliable product.

Images

Firstly, when it comes to pictures, you're trying to not only show off that genetic goodness of yours, but also the type of life you lead or are capable of leading. Images are invitations into our experiences, therefore, use your best ones.

Now I know the algorithms favour dog pics but let's be more original from now on, please.

Some of us are photogenic and some of us aren't, but no matter who you are it's possible to take at least one good picture. Your angles matter guys, the camera doesn't need to be that close to your face and I don't need to see your nose hair.

Additionally, you want to vary your pics. We want to see that you have friends or family that can at least tolerate your presence for the sake of one picture. But also, don't just give us group and family photos that force us to play a game of *Guess Who?* we quite frankly don't have the time or energy to figure out who you are.

Also, be careful with pictures that feature one solo female who looks way too young to be your grandmother, mother or aunt; we'll just assume it's your ex or your current. It's just a bit off putting.

Following on from that...no pictures with exes ever! That's your past, I'm not trying to see that.

Bios

This is the chance where you get to tell us briefly about yourself. Remember that we're looking at you as if you were a product. Now, would you buy something without a description? Typically, no, if you're going to invest your hard-earned money into a product, then you want to know the reason why it's worth it. Now treat yourself like the product and talk about all your best features and no I don't mean your penis (it's probably average anyway).

If you're funny then let us know before we swipe, I'll happily swipe for someone I'm not massively attracted to just because they make me laugh, and I know plenty of girls who do the same.

If you find that you don't have much to say about yourself then that's a bit concerning, you might have to work on your personality a bit before building an online dating profile.

Approach

Now this varies based on what you're looking for. However, even if it's just sex that you want, you should build it up a little – the foreplay before the foreplay. We ladies like to be considered as human beings with feelings and emotions, because that's what we are. When you slide into our DMs, ask us about ourselves before expecting something from us. We don't have to be in love, we don't have to have feels, but you don't have to be cold.

As for the more serious daters out there, put your best forward.

Make us laugh, ask us questions about ourselves, tell us interesting things about you. Reel us in with the cool things about you, let's start the conversation with some vim and vigour. Let's flirt a little but beware you don't overstep the boundaries.

Happy Matching

I'm not trying to suggest that all guys follow this guideline, but it'd be a lot easier to navigate this battlefield if you guys changed things up a little. You can still be yourself within the guidelines as well as help yourself find what you're looking for and save the ladies their time.

The bottom line is that you are capable of doing the same things we do on these apps; you just have to stop being lazy with it.

6

First Date Disasters

There is a tragic but quirky 90s film called 50 First Dates.
Although I don't have amnesia, I have had to approach dating as
if I do, because I would've stopped after several dating disasters.
My bad first date amnesia has meant that I definitely have been
on more than 50 first dates in my lifetime. It's wild when I
think about it because it means that I have provided different
variations of who I am to over 50 people with the hopes that I
vibe with them enough and we continue doing it until something
comes from it.

Writing this as a single woman makes it clear that I have failed
in all 50+ attempts. Actually, I won't be too hard on myself
because it takes 2 to tango just as it does to date. In some of the
situations, I was the one who wasn't interested whilst in others
it was them and for some of them it was mutual.

There are several reasons why dates fail, and nothing comes to
fruition after one. The following is a mixture of scenarios and
testimonials from myself and friends about first dates that we

suffered through with men we most likely never saw again. If you think you have been any of these guys on a date, I hope you now understand why you never saw certain girls again.

This Date is Dead

Sometimes you can get along with someone when typing. It's easier for some guys to be given more time to craft responses. Other times we talk to people who prefer jumping straight into a date, so we pretty much experience them then and there.

Meeting someone in person can be awkward and sometimes people can be shy, however, if you're putting in energy and they're not giving much back then don't feel obliged to stay.

Even when you give the energy, you can't always resurrect the date:

"I once went on a date with a guy who basically had me doing all the talking and it wasn't in a flattering, he asked me loads of questions way, it was because he gave simple closed responses. There wasn't much substance to his answers and a lot of awkward silences were created; that's when my motormouth would come into action because I hate awkward silences. Anyway, it was only a drinks date, so I just pretended I had something to do after. He texted me after saying he's had a great time and that we should do it again...I'm glad he enjoyed the date, but I on the other hand had the life sucked out of me. We didn't have a second date."

He's Throwing a Lot of Red Flags

There's little things people say and do that come across as red flags. If you see the red flags, run baby and I mean that for both parties.

I know that red flags are very subjective, and they'll vary from person to person. There are levels to this shit, so I'm not saying I'll give up on you just because you say '*exetera*' instead of '*etcetera*'. I mean if you're bragging about how often you've cheated in the past and didn't get caught or how you do a lot of crimes, that's when I run. It's a first date, I've only wasted a little bit of time.

There's Something from His Childhood He Needs to Reconcile:

"*Guys should learn to be okay with not being good at things or losing. When it comes to first dates, don't be SUCH a sore loser, especially at something like mini golf. Firstly, we're there to have fun and get to know one another. Secondly, it's not that deep who wins or loses. I once went on a date with a guy that did not take the light-hearted approach to the game. He kept getting annoyed because he was shit and resolved his frustrations by just dragging his golf ball into the hole. Then when we went to count points at the end, including all the holes where he had just put the ball in (which I just let it slide since it was meant to be fun), he counted it wrong. I thought I'd just correct him on the miscount at least, and when I did, he was like 'ooOOOoO someone's competitive! Alright Miss I've got to win.' I was puzzled at his attempt at sarcasm*

as he was the one who'd been cheating the entire time.
Then, he followed his snarky comment with a bitchy one
about me being good at maths because I'm an engineer
so it's not a fair playing field. At this point he'd made
counting up numbers a competition and I was sincerely
over it."

I HATE IT HERE

You ever just been on a date that really sucked in all aspects?
Some dates are like experiencing the seventh circle of hell. These
are the dates where not only are you inconvenienced several
times, there's no care or effort that goes into the date and they
just present undesirable qualities.

There's Quite a Bit to Dissect Here:
"I had been speaking to this guy for a bit and he finally
asked me out one night, I say asked me out, when in
actuality sent me a message saying: 'Come play a game of
mini golf tonight? I have a free game to use' Translation:
HE had a free game, so he went in for free and I paid the
price to go in. On the premise that he invited me on the
date, he could have at least offered to pay my share, but
no...he didn't, sigh. Anyway, after the game of golf, we
went for dinner. He tried my calamari – I don't share
food, but I was trying to be nice – and gagged, stating
that it was revolting. Firstly, calamari are great, your
taste buds need to grow up. Secondly, there was no table
etiquette at his big age. So, after this poor date I decided

not to see him again, however, like men like to do when you're living your best life without them in it, he made an unwarranted return. Unfortunately for him his mother had passed, so I was naturally sympathetic, however, he attempted to use her death to guilt me into being more than friends with him. Now that was a mighty red flag, on top of all the little ones he'd presented before."

Case of The Ex

If you're going to mention her all night long, you might as well bring her along next time. Obviously, the older we get the more experiences and relationships that we have in our past. And whilst it's good to acknowledge the things that happened, talking about an ex for the majority of the first date is a big **no no**.

You need to heal or win her back baby:

"So not only did this guy talk about his ex a lot on our date, he also thought it'd be appropriate to show me photos on his phone of the two of them together. I honestly felt so uncomfortable and didn't know how to respond. I ended up consoling him on his loss. I should've sent him an invoice for the therapy session."

A Usual Spot

There are places that we like to go and things that we like to do. When we start dating people, we usually go to those places and do those things. However, it's problematic if on your first date you mention that you've been to the place before with another person, especially if they didn't ask. It's just not necessary and although it can be forgiven, it's a faux par you can easily avoid by either not opening your mouth or going somewhere different. The choice is yours.

> *Dropped Himself in It:*
> *"On our first date he took me to a place where he'd taken another girl that I knew and disliked. I didn't know this information of course, but he thought to tell me about it on the date and talk about that date. It's safe to say I was a bit salty after that, but I forgave him because he really wasn't used to dating."*

Unnecessarily Uncomfortable

When we go on dates, we typically want to get to know the other person and see how we vibe with them. This means we have to ask questions, give responses and express things that say something about ourselves to the other person.

Unfortunately, sometimes guys will kill the vibe by expressing or doing things that make their dates feel uncomfortable. These statements and actions can vary, for example, talking about other people we don't know in uncouth ways, political or class differences, failure to let us know important information about yourselves, manners in general and more.

A heads up for at least the sake of dress code would've been appreciated:

"I was talking to this guy and it was still early stages. One day he messaged me to tell me to get ready because he was taking me out on a date. I was really excited, and his assertiveness turned me on slightly. So up I got and started to get ready. I wanted to look bomb, so I put on my leopard print bodysuit and a sexy pencil skirt. When I met up with the guy and he was like 'oookkkkkaaaayyy' in a flattering way. Then we headed off to our date location. Please tell me why this boy took me to a church for our first date? I was looking like I'd just come off the pole and he had us together, in CHURCH, praising God, with his family. If things couldn't get more awkward, his grandmother approached me at the end to ask if they'd be seeing me the following week..."

The Dichotomy Between the Silver Spoon and Regular Ones:

"I once went on a date with a guy who was clearly a Tory. He argued with me saying that skiing was cheap. His silver spoon opinions and lifestyle clearly didn't align with mine. He was nice to look at but every time he opened his mouth, I got annoyed. I really should've gotten to know him more before wasting my time and money. I could've saved more to go skiing that year."

He's Threatened by Sexually Liberated Women:

"One guy I went on a date with asked me how many guys I'd slept with. I laughed it off and made a joke, I didn't think the question was warranted at that point. He *paused and waited for me to answer, so I had to let him know that it wasn't any of his business really. As the date progressed, we got quite drunk and he began telling me everything about one of his female friends. It was rather inappropriate as firstly, he was telling her business to a complete stranger and secondly, he was very derogatory towards her, calling her a slag etc. because she dared to explore her sexual freedom. I ignored him mostly and called him rude, and his response was to ask me again about the number of sexual partners I had. Talk about just making a girl feel uncomfortable. It's safe to say I never saw his misogynist ass again!"*

I Prefer My Friends to You:

"One guy decided he'd just tell me that he'd been on a date the night before – good for him, I guess, but I didn't ask. Because of how random it was, I just responded with a direct, 'yeah I don't know what to say to that...' He spent the remainder of our drink trying to convince me that he preferred me, which just made me more uncomfortable. I left after finishing that drink and met my friends at the club instead."

Do We Still Date?

Yes, but infrequently as we're forced to take many breaks. It's a testament to our strength as women to continue trying despite the madness we've found ourselves in. It's tricky trying to figure out how someone will be on a date and we just have to take chances. I've had some wonderful first dates and I'm grateful for the positive experiences because without them I would've given up long ago.

Dating Fatigue

When we start dating, we expect to meet a few people until we find what we want, unless meeting a lot of people is part of the dating agenda. More often than not we experience some atrocious dates and after these dating disasters and not getting any satisfaction, we call it quits. This experience is known as dating fatigue.

Dating is actually a dance that we engage in and it has several steps that we tend to follow in order to execute it well. Now I don't know about you, but repeating the same first steps of a dance really does wear you out.

There's only so much of ourselves that we can keep on giving to hapless men, all to end up disappointed with nothing we want and extras we didn't ask for. That's why sometimes we take breaks from the dating game and allow ourselves to be still. Unfortunately, you lot know how to smell this calm and that's when you usually come sniffing back around.

7

Caught in a Situationship, Because It's Part of the New Norm

It's getting harder and harder to know where you stand with someone.

Given the current dating climate I can safely say that I've been in way more situationships than relationships. Situationships are more common amongst this generation of daters than previous ones. Undefined romantic relationships are the new normal. Where conventional relationships or friends with benefits have more clear guidelines and boundaries, situationships fall into the grey.

We'll often find ourselves in this grey area because we are dealing with men who are afraid of commitment. The types of guys who'll take us out occasionally, invite us over often, tell us they like us but are not ready for a relationship. They'll get jealous of the attention we receive but will refuse to claim us and more often than not, they are keeping their options open – basically, they still belong to the streets.

I understand the appeal of not defining a relationship and alleviating the pressure and accountability that comes with a certain label. It can be a very freeing experience and it can allow you to explore someone at your own pace. However, there's always someone who feels more, wants more or compromises more. There's always someone who is clearer, communicates better and reassures when necessary. Nine times out of ten, it's not the guy.

Undefined romantic relationships can exist and be successful for both parties when there is clear communication, boundaries and expectations set. It's very possible to know where you stand with someone that you're intertwined without a definitive label. Situationships are usually constructed by males who are poor with communication, are scared of commitment or like to play games. The not knowing whether you're coming or going in these intertwinements is probably one of the worst feelings in this dating game.

I do ask that we collectively try and avoid situationships because they're cloudy and clouds usually bring rain and rain is miserable and uncomfortable. If commitment isn't your thing, then maybe you need to think twice before you start connecting with people on a level that goes further than a casual hook-up. If you're a guy who often finds yourself in a situationship, then the chances are you need to communicate better and be as honest and as respectful as you can be to your female counterpart. It's very possible to not define your romantic relationship with a girl, you just need to make sure that you generate some boundaries, check in frequently and be more thoughtful with your words and actions. You'll see that your life will improve because your actions aren't bothering us as much. We're not asking for the world; we're just trying to free up our brain space for more important things.

Going nowhere fast...or at all:
"*My longest situationship lasted about a year. It even had breaks as if we were in a real relationship. I often would ask him what we were doing because I was tired of the dynamic we had. When we'd spend time together it was great, and we'd talk often. We had all the basic ingredients for a relationship, but the commitment wasn't there. I never really knew how single I was when dealing with him. He'd tell me that he still talked to other people, but he didn't like any of them the way he liked me. Then I'd ask him if he would be upset if I talked to other guys, dated other guys, slept with other guys etc. and he'd tell me that it'd upset him, but I was single so I could do what I want. However, if someone popped up on my story and we were looking cosy he'd confront me in a jealous tone. I honestly didn't know whether he was coming or going. At times he'd disappear on me for several weeks or even a month. Other times I'd tell him I couldn't deal with our dynamic anymore, but he'd always sweet talk me and within a few days we'd be back to normal. In the end we had to stop because I couldn't take him ghosting me after sex as frequently as he did.*"

8

There's a Meeting in my Bedroom, And Please Boy Don't Do That...

A big thing in this dating world is sex. We can't ignore how its presence changes a lot of things.

When talking with my ladies on the subject, I've found that far too often we have an array of horror or cringe stories in this department. The bedroom faux pars are not exclusive to habitual lovers, but strangers too. The common themes of these sexual mishaps include boundaries being crossed or not set, or proper etiquette not being adhered to.

Before I dive into a few incidences that my peers and I have experienced, I just wanted to talk a little bit about the approach a lot of have guys to sex. It seems the majority think that they're great, but realistically women haven't been vocal enough about your failures. I have slept with enough men to know that only one in ten of you actually know how to fuck and make it a mutually beneficial experience for your female counterparts for each and every encounter. The rest of you however need a few pointers and some reminders about sex and how to do it well.

I don't know who exactly needs to hear this, but...sex is not a race! And if it were, it definitely wouldn't be a sprint. Finishing as fast as you can isn't the goal; being the Usain Bolt of sex will not win you any gold medals. You should try and take your time with it. Lasting a bit longer wouldn't hurt your cause.

Following on from this, it should be also noted that unlike men, it takes more to get us ladies going. Where you are bullet trains, we are steam engines. You will reach your destination a lot quicker with a lot less effort, then once you reach it, you don't tend to care if we have too. Nine times out of ten we just pretend we have because your lack of attentiveness has probably put us off, so we're content with a quick flick of the bean to get us off whilst you're asleep.

I do know that this qualm we have with you of can be remedied with some clearer communication and removing ego from the bedroom. From your end: you need to allow us to guide you more, listen to us when we say we like or dislike something and not be offended when we give you advice on how to please us. From our end: we need to be more vocal; we need to tell you what we want and what we want is (more) foreplay. We need it for a few reasons 1) If you get us going right, then we're likely to reach our destination. 2) The likelihood of us having an orgasm from penetrative sex alone is highly low - the odds of winning the lottery are higher. 3) The more you do it, the more likely you'll be able to locate the clitoris - I know a lot of you struggle... 4) It's just nice and really makes the difference for a sexual experience.

Sex is supposed to be pleasurable for women. I know you weren't taught this, but it's a fact. Moving forward we need to see sex as a mutually beneficial experience, I'm so over guys giving it the talk without having mastered the walk.

Speaking of talk, I just wanted to add that the way in which some guys approach sex is very off putting and really makes us not want to sleep with you at all. It's fine to only want sex from someone, I can admit that I have used several of you to (attempt to) satisfy my needs here and there. However, the impersonal, *you're just a sex object* approach is self-sabotage at best. Treat us nicely, we can sleep with you and not catch feelings; there's no need to be rude to us in order to prevent feels. Additionally, stop expecting us to just send you nudes just because you asked. You need to stop with your entitlement and treat us fairly going into the bedroom. Remember our stimulation matters too.

He Did What?

The following is just a collection of stories where men made us feel uncomfortable, weirded out, embarrassed or whatever as a result of their bedroom antics or attitudes towards sex.

Who do you love:
   "We had been speaking for about a month before we met. The first date went well, and it resulted in him coming back to mine. One thing led to another and we had sex. It was all going well until he came and said he

loved me as he did. That was really awkward."

A heads up would have been nice:
"There was a guy I was dating casually and on this particular occasion we went to his after a boozy date. We had sex as usual and after we finished, I went to the bathroom and then came back out to him having set up his LOUD sleeping ventilator, put on his eye mask and fallen fast asleep, snoring and everything. He hadn't warned me of his set-up before inviting me back to his or even bothered to wait for me to come back in before nodding off. Talk about a lack of manners."

Runaway baby before he puts his kids in you:
"My personal favourite was a guy who refused to wear a condom and told me that if anything happened, it was only a little pill I'd have to take and that it was 'free anyway'. His total disregard for sexual health and safety had me out of there in seconds."

Choke me daddy, but not that hard:
"A former partner and I, back when we were together decided we wanted to spice up our sex life and try new things. We agreed to try choking, we had our safe word arranged and we were ready to go. Given it was our first go, I thought he'd be a bit gentler, but alas I was wrong and too cowardly to use the safe word so instead I passed out."

Don't overdo the Dutch courage:
"I'd had a period of celibacy and I was ready to get back

into the game. Lucky for me my friend had a friend who was fit and at a party, he managed to set us up. When we went back to mine that's when the accumulation of everything he had drunk hit him, as he projectile vomited on my back and all over my bed. I had to call in my friends to help with sorting out the mess – basically discarding my bedding completely. After that was sorted, we decided it was best he go home and he left my house topless, holding what he thought was his t-shirt, by instead was my pillowcase. All I wanted was sex, but instead I got humiliation and lost my bedding."

More than a weird flex, not okay:
   "Not actually anything to do with the sex, but he put on creepypasta after we slept together because he said it helped him get to sleep…"

I said we like foreplay, so make sure you include us too:
   "I one went back with this one guy I'd met in poetry and spoken work society. He was this cool avant garde type and I was ready to see what he could do in bed. When we got to his room, he put on a film, Limitless. Then we started making out and doing some bits. We got the point of putting on the condom and I was ready for him to put it in, but he had one of those moments where it stopped being hard because of it. I wasn't going to have sex with him without it, I suggested that I help him get it back up with my skills, but he said to me: 'Let me sort myself out for a second and I'll let you know when I'm ready.' Young, naive me just said sure and directed my eyes towards the film as he wanked himself off next to

me. About two minutes later he let out shriek letting me know he had orgasmed and I just sat there in disbelief. He didn't even offer to satisfy me in any other way to make up for his solo act. We just slept in silence and I left as early as I could once the Uber surge prices had gone down. I haven't watched the film Limitless since."

9

Conclusion

It should be obvious that this isn't directed at every heterosexual man that exists, but I'll just say it anyway...this isn't directed at all men. If you don't find yourself represented within these situations and stories, then you're probably, who I and a lot of other ladies are looking for. It's just taking us a while to meet because of all the shit we're wading through.

Overall, there's a message in here somewhere for the boys and hopefully some entertainment for the girls. Sometimes we're really not asking for the world and men drive us mad with their actions. At the end of the day it's not just about one party, it's about both. Let's make our exchanges fair so that we can be a bit more satisfied in this world of dating.

Now that you know better, do better.

Epilogue

Hell hath no fury like a woman scorned.

Afterword

Thank you to all the wonderful ladies who have shared their stories with me and allowed me to share them with the world. Even after all of that mess, we're all still standing and still have the capacity to love.

Printed in Great Britain
by Amazon